Country ABCs

India ABCs

by Marcie Aboff
illustrated by Frances Moore

A Book About the People and Places of India

Special thanks to our advisers for their expertise:

Haimanti Banerjee, Outreach Coordinator
South Asia Center, University of Pennsylvania

Susan Kesselring, M.A., Literacy Educator
Rosemount–Apple Valley–Eagan (Minnesota) School District

PICTURE WINDOW BOOKS
Minneapolis, Minnesota

Editor: Jill Kalz
Designer: Nathan Gassman
Page Production: Tracy Kaehler
Creative Director: Keith Griffin
Editorial Director: Carol Jones
The illustrations in this book were created digitally.

Picture Window Books
5115 Excelsior Boulevard
Suite 232
Minneapolis, MN 55416
877-845-8392
www.picturewindowbooks.com

Printed in the United States of America.

Library of Congress Cataloging-in-Publication Data
Aboff, Marcie.
India ABCs : a book about the people and places of India / by Marcie Aboff ;
illustrated by Frances Moore.
p. cm. — (Country ABCs)
Includes bibliographical references and index.
ISBN 1-4048-1571-6 (hardcover)
1. India—Juvenile literature. 2. Alphabet books. I. Moore, Frances, ill.
II. Title. III. Series.
DS407.A54 2005
954—dc22   2005021814

Namaskar! (nah-mus-kar)

That's how people greet each other in India. They often put their palms together and bow, too. Bowing is their way of saying, "I respect you." India is a country in southern Asia. It sits on a large peninsula. India is about one-third the size of the United States, but it has about three times as many people. More than 1 billion people live in India. Only China has more people than India.

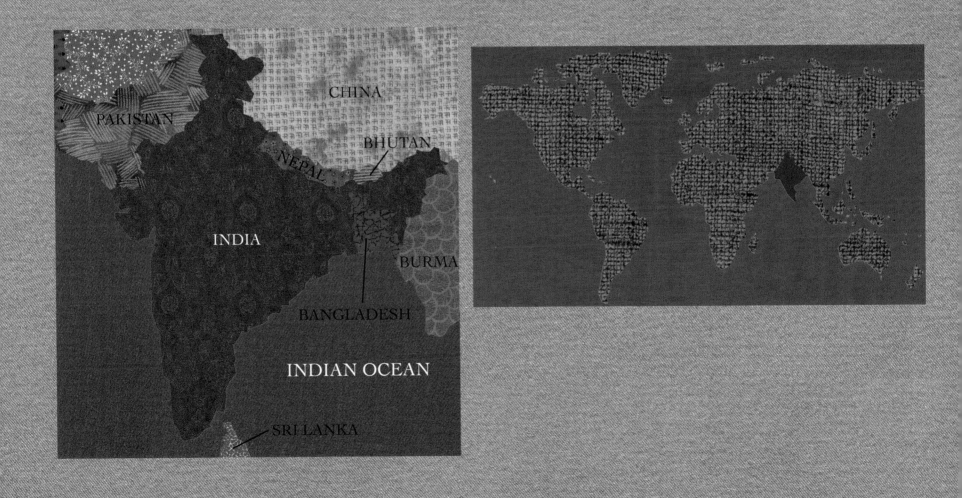

A is for art.

There are many kinds of paintings in India. Some are filled with religious images. These paintings show gods and goddesses. Others are based on everyday life and folk tradition. These paintings show people working, dancing, and doing other common activities.

FAST FACT: In many Indian families, a bride's hands and feet are painted with beautiful, black designs the night before her wedding. These designs are called *mehndi* (mehn-di). Overnight, the black color dries and turns red. Red is said to bring good luck.

B is for British India.

India became a part of the British Empire in 1876. But even before that, the British had a lot of control over India. The British East India Company had already been gathering land and power in India for 200 years. Eventually, the Indians fought for their independence, and, in 1947, leaders from India and Great Britain agreed to divide the country into two. One part was called India, and the other part was called Pakistan.

C is for cricket.

Cricket is a popular and exciting sport in India. It is a ball-and-bat game played by two teams, each with 11 members. The British brought cricket to India more than 250 years ago.

FAST FACT: India's cricket team won its first big victory in international cricket in 1983. That year, it beat the West Indies cricket team and claimed the Prudential World Cup.

D is for Diwali (di-waa-li).

Diwali is one of India's most celebrated festivals. It is often called the Festival of Lights. Diwali is a celebration of wealth, good luck, and the victory of good over evil. During Diwali, people decorate their houses and streets with lights.

E is for elephant.

Indian elephants are important parts of Indian culture. They are often decorated with gold and jewels and are used in religious and festive processions. One of the Hindu gods, Ganesha, has an elephant head. Hindus worship him as the remover of obstacles.

FAST FACT: Indian elephants live in forests and jungles. They have smaller ears than African elephants.

F is for flag.

The Indian flag is orange, white, and green. Orange stands for bravery, white stands for truth, and green stands for faith. In the center of the flag is a blue wheel. The wheel stands for progress and holy law.

G is for Ganges River.

The Ganges River is one of the longest rivers in the world. It is considered sacred to most Indian people. They believe the river has the power to wash away their sins. Some people have their ashes scattered in the Ganges River after they die.

H is for Himalayas.

Many scientists believe that India was once a part of a large piece of land that drifted north and crashed into Asia. They believe the crash created the Himalayas. The Himalayas are the highest mountains in the world. They stretch about 1,500 miles (2,400 kilometers) across northern India.

FAST FACT: The tops of the Himalayas are covered with snow all year long. The word *Himalaya* means "House of Snow."

I is for Indus Valley.

The Indus Valley was the home of the first people of India. Archeologists have uncovered objects dating back to around 2500 B.C. These objects include well-built houses, paved streets, decorated pottery, and writing tablets.

J is for Jawaharlal Nehru.

Jawaharlal Nehru worked hard to help India win its independence in 1947. That same year, he became the country's first prime minister. Nehru encouraged the use of technology. Many factories and roads were built in India under his leadership.

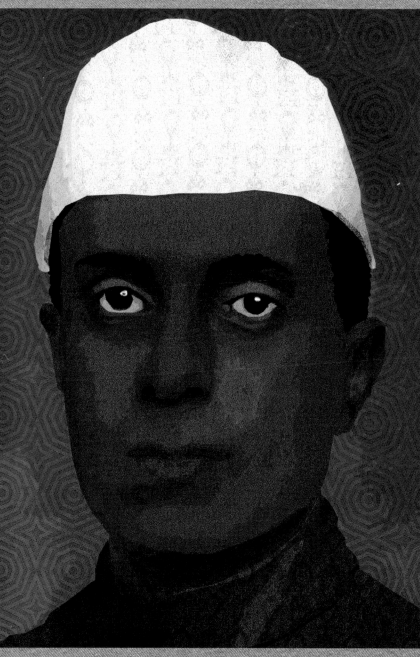

K is for karma.

Karma is the belief that a person's behavior affects his or her path in life. Doing good deeds will bring a good life. Doing bad deeds, however, will not only bring a bad life but also a bad afterlife (life after death). Most Indians believe in karma.

L is for languages.

Hindi is the national language of India, but the government recognizes 14 other official languages as well. In addition, hundreds of dialects are spoken. In schools, both Hindi and English are usually taught.

अ a

आ ā

ई i

ए e

ओ o

ऋ r̥

उ u

ई ī

औ au

अ a

अ ah

ऋ r̥

प pa

पी pi

M is for Mohandas "Mahatma" Gandhi.

Mohandas "Mahatma" Gandhi helped India win its freedom from Great Britain. Gandhi protested peacefully against things he believed were wrong. His picture is on an Indian banknote.

FAST FACT: Gandhi's peaceful ways and strong will earned him the name "Mahatma," which means "Great Soul."

N is for new Hollywood.

India has one of the largest movie industries in the world. More than 800 films are made each year in Mumbai (formerly Bombay). This lively, moviemaking city has been closely compared to Hollywood, California. Mumbai is often called "Bollywood" (Bombay plus Hollywood).

O is for Odissi (oh–diss–i).

The *Odissi* dance is a traditional dance form from eastern India. Flowing and graceful, it is usually based on religious themes. The *Bharatnatyam* (bhaarath-naat-yum) dance from southern India is another well-known traditional Indian dance.

P is for parantha
(paar-aan-tha).

Parantha is a flat bread from northern India. Sometimes, the parantha is filled with vegetables. Another kind of flat, Indian bread is called *naan* (niahn). This flat bread is baked in a hot clay oven called a tandoor.

FAST FACT: Instead of using forks and spoons, many Indians eat with the fingers of their right hand.

Q is for quarry.

A quarry is a large, open pit from which stones are mined. Indian quarries produce large amounts of sandstone, granite, slate, and marble. These beautiful stones are exported to countries around the world for use in homes and businesses.

R is for railroad.

The railroad system is very important in India. Trains are a cheap method of transportation for millions of Indians. Trains also carry two-thirds of the nation's freight.

FAST FACT: India's "Palace-on-Wheels" luxury train has been called one of the best luxury trains in the world.

S is for saris.

Saris are the traditional clothing worn by Hindu women in India. Usually made of cotton or silk, saris come in thousands of colors and designs. Each area of the country has its own designs. The most expensive saris are sewn with threads of real gold or silver. Women wear saris in different ways, depending on the region in which they live.

FAST FACT: Many Indian men wear dhotis. A dhoti is a piece of white cotton wrapped around the body. One or both ends are brought through the legs and tucked into the waistband.

T is for Taj Mahal.

The Taj Mahal was built in the mid-1600s. The emperor Shah Jahan had it built in memory of his beloved wife. Her tomb lies inside. Made mostly of white marble, the building took 20,000 workers more than 20 years to complete. Some people call it the "Eighth Wonder of the World."

U is for untouchables.

Indian society was once divided into groups called castes. Very educated people were in the highest caste. Workers were in the lowest caste. Some people were even below the lowest caste. They were called "untouchables." They did the dirty and difficult jobs that no one else wanted.

V is for villages.

About 500,000 villages are scattered throughout India. Villages range from groups of huts to modern stone and brick houses. In most cases, fewer than 1,000 people live in a village. Most villagers are farmers.

W is for winners.

India's international award winners include Mother Teresa and Rabindranath Tagore. Mother Teresa received the Nobel Peace Prize in 1979. She was a nun who took care of the poor and sick in Kolkata (formerly Calcutta). Author Rabindranath Tagore was the first Indian ever to receive a Nobel Prize in literature (1913).

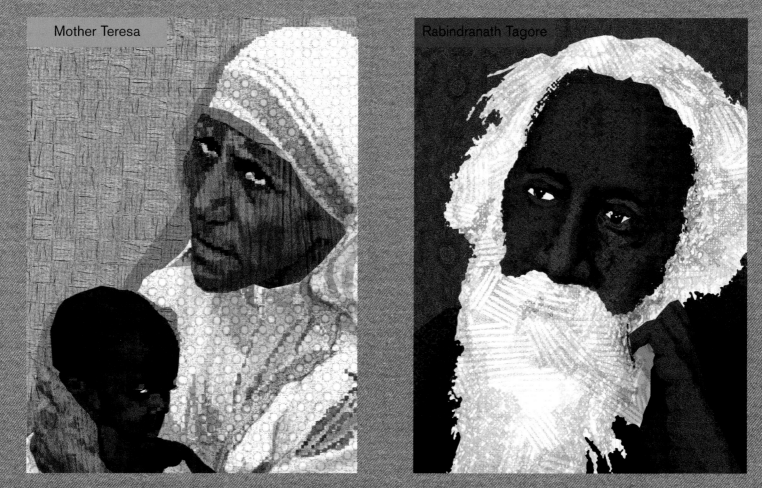

Mother Teresa

Rabindranath Tagore

FAST FACT: Film director Satyajit Ray received an honorary Academy Award in 1992. He made his films in Bengali (the language of eastern India), but their touching stories were understood and loved by people around the world.

X is for extremes.

India is a land of extremes. Its landscape includes snow-capped mountains, deserts, rain forests, and wide, sandy beaches. Its people practice many religions and speak several languages. While some Indians are wealthy, many are very poor.

Y is for yoga.

Yoga has been practiced in India for thousands of years. It is based on the idea that the mind and body are one. People who do yoga use meditation and exercise to help improve and maintain their health.

FAST FACT: People all around the world practice yoga. Some schools teach yoga to help children build strong bodies and sharp minds.

Z is for zebu.

The zebu is a kind of humped cattle that originated in India. It is thought to be the world's oldest domesticated cattle. Indians use the zebu for transportation and to pull carts.

FAST FACT: India has more cattle than any other country. Cattle are used for plowing and to make dairy products such as milk and butter.

India in Brief

Official name: Republic of India

Capital: New Delhi

Official language: Hindi is the national language, but the Indian government recognizes several other official languages as well.

Population: 1 billion

People: About 72 percent of all Indians are Indo-Aryans who live in northwestern and central India; 25 percent are Dravidians from southern India; and the remaining 3 percent are Mongoloids.

Main religions: 80 percent Hindu; other religious groups include Buddhism, Muslim, Sikhism, and Christianity

Education: Education is provided through public and private schools. But poverty and the need to support their families forces many children to drop out at a young age. About half of the population cannot read or write.

Major holidays: Republic Day (January 26), Holi (March; celebrates the coming of spring), Independence Day (August 15), Diwali (October or November; the Festival of Lights)

Transportation: trains, buses, bicycles, motorbikes

Area: 1,269,345 square miles (3,287,590 square kilometers)

Highest point: Kanchenjunga, 28,208 feet (8,598 meters)

Lowest point: Trivandrum, sea level

Climate: India has three seasons: cool, hot, and wet. The rainy season is between June and September. During this time, strong winds called monsoons bring large amounts of rain to India.

Type of government: India is the largest federal republic, or democracy, in the world.

Head of government: prime minister

Major industries: steel, machinery, chemicals, computer software, filmmaking

Natural resources: coal, iron ore, bauxite, natural gas, diamonds, farmland

Major agricultural products: rice, wheat, cotton, tea, water buffalo, sheep, fish

Chief exports: gems and jewelry, textile and leather goods, chemicals, stone

Money: Indian rupee

Say It in HINDI

hello . . . . .namaste (nah-mus-tay) or namaskar (nah-mus-kar)

please (formal use) . . . . .kripaya (kri-pa-yaa)

thank you (formal use) . . . . .dhanyavad (thon-ya-vaad)

yes . . . . .ji ha (gee haa)

no . . . . .ji nahi (gee nhee)

how are you? . . . . .ap kaisile hai? (aap kas-ay hay)

best wishes! . . . . .shubh kamnae! (shub kam-nhi)

Glossary

archaeologists–people who study human life from long ago

dialect–a different way of speaking the same language

domesticated–tamed; no longer wild

freight–goods that are shipped from one place to another

Hindus–followers of a religion called Hinduism, the main religion of India

meditation–thinking deeply and quietly

peninsula–a piece of land with water on three sides

processions–groups of people moving in an orderly way

protesting–showing disapproval

revolt–to fight against one's own government or group

sacred–dedicated or reserved for the worship of a god

To Learn More

At the Library

Italia, Bob. *India.* Edina, Minn.: Abdo Publishing, 2002.

Park, Ted. *Taking Your Camera to India.* Austin, Texas: Steadwell Books, 2001.

Srinivasan, Radhika, and Leslie Jermyn. *India.* New York: Marshall Cavendish, 2002.

On the Web

FactHound offers a safe, fun way to find Internet sites related to this book. All of the sites on FactHound have been researched by our staff.

1. Visit *www.facthound.com*
2. Type in this special code for age-appropriate sites: 1404815716
3. Click on the FETCH IT button.

Your trusty FactHound will fetch the best sites for you!

Index

LOOK FOR ALL OF THE BOOKS IN THE COUNTRY ABCS SERIES: